I0846142

The Roadmap to Constructing Wealth

The Step-by-Step Guide to Wealth Accumulation and the Power of Smart Money Management

By

Edward J. young

The roadmap to constructing wealth

TABLE OF CONTENT

Introduction 4

Chapter 1...6
Make your credit card better. 6
Chapter 2..45
Outsmart the banks 45
Chapter 3..62
Prepare to make an investment...........................62
Chapter 4..76
Making a financial plan..................................76
Chapter 5..88
saving when sleeping....................................88
Chapter 6..93
Investing is not limited to the wealthy. 93
Chapter 7...101
How to Keep and Grow Your Financial System...........101
Chapter 8...109
A life of gold 109

Introduction

There is a less-traveled path that offers the appeal of financial freedom, security, and prosperity in the middle of life's busy crossroads, among the din of bills, dreams, everyday expenses, and future uncertainty. However, how can you navigate this way through the chaos? How do you make your way through its curves and turns, its hills and valleys, to arrive at the desired location of genuine wealth? "The Roadmap to Constructing Wealth," your guide, is your welcome.

Everybody wants to live a comfortable life without having to worry about how much money they have. However, creating money is like creating a tower it requires more than just raw materials it also requires a strategy, a plan, and a roadmap.

This book is about establishing a life of abundance and financial peace, not simply about real estate, stocks, or money. It's about finding the delicate balance between living in the moment and making plans for the future.

"The Roadmap to Constructing Wealth" is ready to change your financial situation decision by decision, piece by piece, by fusing tried-and-true methods with up-to-date financial knowledge.

Are you prepared to travel to a place where riches are more than just money but a total sense of well-being, where every choice you make brings you closer to your objective and where money works for you? Flip the page and set out on a path toward an infinitely promising future.

Chapter 1

Make your credit card better.

It is crucial for figuring out creditworthiness. This ratio is used by credit bureaus and lenders to evaluate an individual's capacity for responsible credit management. A lower percentage improves credit scores and denotes prudent money management, which makes these borrowers more desirable to lenders. On the other side, because a large ratio indicates possible financial risk, it may result in poorer credit ratings.

A sound credit profile allows you to access more loan possibilities down the road, so it's vital to understand the credit utilization ratio. By using credit wisely and maintaining modest credit card balances, people can improve their creditworthiness.

The Credit Utilization Ratio, which shows the percentage of available credit that is used, is a crucial indicator in personal finance.

The roadmap to constructing wealth

Comprehending and effectively handling credit use can have a substantial effect on credit scores, which in turn can affect how financially responsible lenders view us.

We practice responsible credit management by keeping our utilization ratio low, which enhances our creditworthiness and finally results in better loan conditions.

1. Combination and Explanation

A basic credit score statistic called the credit utilization ratio indicates what proportion of a person's available credit they are currently using.

This ratio, which is calculated by dividing the total amount of credit account balances due by the total amount of credit limits, is crucial for determining creditworthiness and offers insight into a person's credit management practices.

Gaining better financial prospects and preserving a positive credit profile depends on your ability to comprehend and manage this ratio.

Because it shows responsible credit usage and might raise one's credit score, a lower credit utilization ratio typically around 30% is regarded as good.

Recipe

Take a look at the following example to see how the Credit Utilization Ratio is calculated:

Paul, for instance, possesses a single credit card with a $100,000 credit limit and a $30,000 balance at present.

Credit Utilization Ratio = (Total Outstanding Balances) / (Total Credit Limits) * 100 = (30,000) / (100,000) * 100 = 30% is the formula for calculating credit utilization ratios.

Justification

Paul's credit utilization ratio in this instance is 30%, meaning he is making use of 30% of his $100,000 credit limit. This ratio is calculated as a percentage by dividing his total amount of debt ($30,000) by the credit limit ($100,000).

It is usually accepted that Paul is using credit responsibly and isn't maxing out his credit card when his credit usage ratio is 30% or lower. Keeping your credit utilization ratio low is a wise financial move.

2. The credit utilization ratio's importance

Because it indicates how well someone manages their credit, credit usage is a significant component in credit rating. It's just the ratio of the credit they have available to them to the credit they are using. Their credit score may suffer if they have a high credit usage ratio, which indicates they are utilizing a significant amount of their credit. This is because it may indicate they are depending too much on credit.

Conversely, a low credit utilization ratio might help someone's credit score because it shows that they have a strong income-to-expense ratio. Low usage is preferred by lenders since it indicates that borrowers are not taking on excessive debt and are, therefore, less likely to be dangerous borrowers.

Real-life scenario

Statistics highlight how important it is to maintain a healthy credit utilization ratio.

For example, those with low usage ratios (below 30%) have better credit scores and are more likely to be eligible for credit card and loan interest rates that are lower.

Conversely, people with high usage ratios could find it harder to get credit or pay higher interest rates.

A brighter and more stable financial future can be attained by managing credit properly, as evidenced by statistics showing a strong correlation between responsible credit usage and enhanced financial well-being.

3. How Do You Use Your Credit When You Have Two Credit Cards?

We'll look at how the credit usage ratio is calculated in the case of someone who has two credit cards. Allow me to explain the specific matter at hand.

• The First Card has a ten-year credit history and a $10 credit limit, and the user typically keeps the credit limit on this card at 15%.

The roadmap to constructing wealth

• The Second Card has a credit history of just one month, and it has a $.1.4 credit limit as well as a 70% credit limit.

This example will demonstrate responsible credit management and teach us how to compute the credit utilization ratio of a person with multiple credit cards.

Let's first work out how to calculate the use ratio of several cards.

Worksheet

When determining the credit usage ratio for a person with multiple credit cards, we first compute the ratio for each card individually before calculating the total ratio based on the aggregate credit limits and outstanding balances on both cards:

1. The credit limit on the first card is $1,000,000. 15% Credit Utilization (usually kept up to date by the individual). First Card Credit Utilization = 15% of $1,000,000 = $150,000.

2. Credit Utilization on the Second Card:

70% of the Credit Limit of $140,000 (usually maintained by the cardholder); Credit Utilization on the Second Card = 70% of $140,000 = 98,000

Now, let's calculate the credit usage ratio as a whole:

• The total outstanding balance on both cards is $150,000 on the first card and $98,000 on the second, totaling $248,000.

• The total credit limit is $1,000,000 for the first card and $140,000 for the second card, totaling $1,140,000.

• Total Credit Limits / Total Outstanding Balances = $248,000 / $1,140,000 * 100 = 21.75%

The person is using roughly 21.75% of their total credit limit on both cards in this instance, which is equivalent to their overall credit utilization of 21.75%.

Impact on Credit Score

We now understand how a person with several credit cards' credit usage ratio is determined for assessing their credit rating.

One credit card's utilization percentage is clearly within permissible bounds, but the person's overall credit utilization is 21.75%. On the other hand, the second credit card is occasionally overused.

Lenders and credit scoring algorithms frequently view low overall credit usage favorably; even if a person has a greater use ratio on one credit card, the fact that their total credit utilization is still low suggests that they are managing their credit responsibly.

Even if a high utilization ratio on a single card could have some effect on credit score, if the user maintains a low overall use ratio, the total effect might not be that great. One's credit rating is also greatly influenced by other elements, such as timely payments and a clean credit history.

4. Is a credit usage rate of 0% good?

Even if it would seem like a prudent way to have 0% credit utilization, it might not be the best for your credit score. In general, it is better to have some credit usage, ideally between 1% and 10%. When you have 0% credit utilization, you are not using any of your available credit, which might not give creditors enough information to determine whether you are creditworthy.

Creditors look for proof that you can use credit responsibly, such as when you use it and pay it back on schedule. A low credit usage rate makes you a more desirable borrower because it indicates that you are using credit but aren't becoming unduly dependent on it.

By consistently paying off credit card balances in full and handling your bills sensibly, you can maintain a low but not zero credit utilization rate and enhance your financial situation.

5. Typical Myths Regarding Credit Utilization

I'd like to clear up some common myths and fallacies regarding credit use and credit score because understanding them can help you manage your credit more wisely. To shed light on these key ideas, let's dispel a few misconceptions:

The credit score is raised by canceling unused credit cards. To be clear, closing credit cards that you don't use can lower your credit score because it lowers the total amount of credit you have accessible, which could lead to a higher credit use rate. Consequently, maintaining the open status of previous credit cards, especially those with no annual fees contributes to a lengthier credit history and ultimately raises credit scores.

Good credit is only available to those with high earnings.

To be clear, credit scores are determined by credit history rather than income. A larger salary can aid in managing debt, but anyone can attain an outstanding credit score by practicing responsible credit behavior. Regardless of income, timely bill payments and maintaining low credit card balances are critical components of excellent credit building.

It damages your credit to check your credit score.

To be clear there is no impact on your credit when you check your credit score (a soft inquiry). However, when you apply for new credit (a hard inquiry), your credit score may temporarily decline.

Your credit score is raised when you have a balance on your credit card. To be clear, having a balance does not raise your credit rating. Nonetheless, you can raise your credit score by making all of your monthly credit card payments on time.

Briefly

Multiple credit card holders can enhance their credit ratings and general financial health by being proactive in maintaining a low overall credit utilization rate.

Maintaining a low ratio shows prospective lenders that you are managing your credit responsibly. The credit utilization ratio is a significant component of credit rating.

The following are some ways that people can achieve this goal:

1. Keep an eye on your credit card balances and try to keep them as low as possible.
   Even if it means dividing up your expenses across multiple cards, try not to max out your credit cards.

2. Pay Credit Card Bills in Full and On Time: To avoid paying hefty interest and late fees, always pay credit card bills in full and on time. Making your payments on time has a big impact on your creditworthiness and credit history.

3. Avoid Opening Multiple Credit Cards at Once: Getting multiple credit cards opened simultaneously could lead to harsh queries and a lower average account age. Instead, think about getting more credit as needed.

4. Use Old Credit Cards Responsibly: Rather than closing down old, unused credit cards, think about using them sometimes for modest purchases and paying off the balance right away. This will help you keep a longer credit history and raise your credit score.

By following these guidelines, you can actively control your credit utilization ratio and observe improvements in these credit scores. Along with raising credit ratings, a low credit utilization ratio also makes loans with better conditions, cheaper interest rates, and credit limits more accessible.

Tricks to beat credit card companies at their own game

The average American has three credit cards, according to Experian data; Gen Z consumers have an average of 1.8 cards, while Baby Boomers have an average of 4.8 cards. The average credit card load for Americans, according to another Experian data, is $5,589 in value. When you are unable to pay off your credit card bill, it is simple to get into debt, but there are strategies to get out of this situation.

What is the cost to you of using your credit cards?

Have you ever taken the time to figure out how much you are losing to your credit cards? The outcomes could surprise you. Let's say you have three credit cards, for instance. The first has a debt of $4,000 at 18% interest, the second has a balance of $7,000 at 19% interest, and the third has a total of $3,500 at 20% interest. This equates to a $14,500 total debt with an average interest rate of 19%.

To make things easier, figure out the total amount owing and average interest for each of the three cards separately.

Then, imagine that you wish to pay off the $14,500 in three years.

In this instance, your monthly payment would be $531.51, and you would pay $4634.44 in interest on a $14.500 total balance nearly thirty-two percent of your whole debt total.

Taking against companies who issue credit cards

If you're sick of paying astronomical interest on your credit card debts, don't give up. With the right strategy and a lot of self-control, you can beat the credit card companies. It's critical to understand how to manage multiple cards effectively.

Acknowledge "islands"

The "island approach" calls for allocating a distinct category of purchases to each credit card. Rewards are a feature of many cards; some give you cash back at the gas pump, while others give you points for groceries. You may receive 6% cash back on groceries, 3% cash back on select department store purchases, 5% cash back on gas purchases, and perhaps 2% cash back on everything else, depending on the credit card.

Although this is a sensible credit card usage strategy, read the fine print and exercise caution. Even though there might be an initial sign-up incentive for just one card, it might not be sufficient to cover the annual cost. Having the greatest rewards card for each category of significant expenditures and paying the entire bill down each month are the long-term goals.

Having several credit cards can lead to issues.

Credit cards can cause more harm than good if they are not used responsibly. Take into account your history of on-time payments when applying for a new credit card, and be cautious not to overextend yourself. When managing several credit cards, it's crucial to take your financial condition into account since strategy and discipline are crucial when utilizing techniques such as the island approach.

The drawbacks of possessing several credit cards

In the future, if you plan to purchase a new car or get a mortgage, keeping your credit in good standing will be essential to getting approved and securing the greatest interest rate.

You might not notice any issues with your credit card right now, but later on, when you want to make a big purchase, you might notice a little increase in interest. For instance, you would pay thousands of dollars in additional interest throughout the loan if you obtained a mortgage with a rate that was half a point higher because of your credit history.

Engage in a game of credit card balance transfer.

Another option to get even with credit card companies is through balance transfers. These days, almost all credit card companies provide balance transfer cards with 0% interest for a certain period. You might pay off your debt more quickly by transferring the balances on any high-interest credit cards to a new card, where you would pay no interest for six to twenty-one months.

The ideal course of action is to pay off your debt in full within the interest-free introductory period; if that isn't feasible, you can transfer the balance from the new card to another 0% interest card.

The roadmap to constructing wealth

You might avoid paying interest for 36 months if you did this with three distinct cards, each of which had a 12-month 0% introductory rate. However, this isn't the best course of action because all of those transfers could hurt your credit score.

The hidden benefits of your card

• Even though cash back and points are common credit card benefits, there are a few less well-known benefits that might be quite helpful.

• Extended warranties, purchase protection, and cell phone protection are offered by many card issuers to their customers, but not all of them take advantage of these advantages.

• A lot of travel credit cards also come with perks like insurance against trip cancellation or interruption, luggage protection, and even access to airport lounges that are designed to lessen the stress of traveling.

Whether you're searching for a student credit card or a new travel rewards card, you might want to investigate the benefits that each card provides.

The benefits offered by a card issuer and card can differ significantly at times, so it's important to review the terms and conditions before applying.

For instance, access to airport lounges or travel insurance may make the yearly cost of a credit card beneficial if you are a regular traveler. A no-annual-fee cash-back card could be helpful if all you're searching for is a regular spending card because it can provide longer warranties and purchase protection.

In light of this, the following are a few little-known (but crucial) credit card features, along with a list of the best credit cards that include these benefits.

Insurance against delayed or canceled travel

Bad weather can cause your flight to be delayed or canceled, or you could have to interrupt your vacation because of uncontrollable conditions. Credit card travel insurance could come in handy if you find yourself in a position where you have a non-refundable airline ticket that you won't be able to use.

Coverage is provided by trip cancellation and interruption insurance for every time you pay for certain travel expenses with an eligible credit card. Your travel expenses, including those that are non-refundable through the provider, may be returned up to a specific amount if your trip is canceled or delayed due to circumstances beyond your control.

I suggest the following top credit cards with trip cancellation/interruption insurance:

• Chase Sapphire Preferred Card: This card offers up to $10,000 in trip cancellation and interruption coverage per person and up to $20,000 per trip in qualifying circumstances. It also covers non-refundable, prepaid travel expenses including hotels, airline, and tour packages.

• American Express Platinum Card: Up to $10,000 in trip cancellation and interruption insurance and up to $20,000 in non-refundable travel expenses are provided every 12 months for qualifying circumstances and events (additional limitations apply).

Ink Business Preferred Credit Card: Up to $5,000 in prepaid, non-refundable travel expenses per person and $10,000 per covered trip may be covered by trip cancellation and interruption insurance under certain conditions and occurrences.

Baggage protection

There's nothing more annoying than reaching your destination and finding your luggage nowhere to be found. You will probably have to cut short your trip to deal with any missing or delayed bags (such as a fast drive to the closest store to replace clothing and toiletries).

Many travel credit cards come with features that are meant to reduce some of the anxiety associated with traveling. For example, most luggage protection features cover your bags if they are misplaced or delayed by the carrier; if they are lost forever, coverage will pay you back for the full cost of your misplaced luggage up to a certain amount.

The following are a few top picks for credit cards that offer luggage insurance:

• Chase Sapphire Reserve: Coverage for the principal cardholder and an immediate family member up to $3,000 in lost or damaged luggage reimbursement for each passenger (by the carrier).

• Capital One Venture X Rewards Credit Card: New York residents may receive up to $2,000 in reimbursement for each bag lost or damaged by the carrier and up to $3,000 in total lost luggage reimbursement per covered trip.

• Bank of America Travel Rewards credit card: Check your card's benefits handbook for more details. If it's a Visa Signature card, you might be qualified for reimbursement for misplaced luggage.

First-class boarding and free checked baggage

If you've ever been upgraded when traveling, you know how convenient it is to board an aircraft early. This allows you to have more time to relax before takeoff and avoid battling for space in the overhead bin for your carry-on luggage.

Priority boarding and free checked bags are two benefits of many popular co-branded airline credit cards. Depending on the card, you may even be able to utilize the free checked-bag incentive to cover more than one bag, including luggage for other passengers who are scheduled to travel with you.

Here are a few best choices for credit cards that come with free checked luggage and priority boarding:

• Delta SkyMiles Platinum American Express Card: Offers free first checked bag and priority boarding in Main Cabin 1 for the cardholder and up to nine additional passengers traveling on the same ticket on Delta flights.

• Citi / AAdvantage Platinum Select World Elite MasterCard: Offers the cardholder and up to four companions on the same reservation a free first-checkd bag and preferential boarding on qualifying American Airlines flights.

Availability of airport lounges

Although hanging around an airport isn't the most comfortable thing to do, it can be worthwhile if you have a few hours to spare before your departure and have access to an airport lounge. Instead of waiting in line at the gate, airport lounges can be a nice spot to wait for your flight. Most lounges also offer free snacks, beverages, and Wi-Fi.

Airport lounge memberships are available to everyone, but you might be able to enter for free if you have the appropriate credit card. Airport lounge access is a common feature of premium travel cards, and occasionally, this benefit includes admission for your traveling friends as well. In other cases, traveling companions are welcome, although there is a charge.

I suggest the following credit cards as some of the best ones that offer access to airport lounges:

• Chase Sapphire Reserve: Free access to more than 1,300 VIP airport lounges in more than 500 cities worldwide with Priority Pass Select membership.

• Capital One Venture X Rewards Credit Card: You and two guests will have unlimited access to over 1,300

Priority Pass Select lounges as well as Capital One lounges.

• American Express Platinum Card: Provides access to the Global Lounge Collection, which includes more than 1,400 lounges spread over 650 locations across the globe.

Collision damage waiver for rental cars

Renting a car is essential whether you're going on a business or pleasure trip. Auto rental coverage is often included with credit cards, and it might be main or secondary. If you decline the motor rental company's insurance, you usually have the option to purchase a collision damage waiver, which provides main insurance coverage.

In view, the following credit cards offer some of the best rental car insurance:

• Chase Sapphire Preferred: You will receive primary rental coverage against theft and collision damage up to the car's actual cash value when you decline the rental company's insurance and charge the rental to your card.

This benefit applies to the majority of rental cars both domestically and abroad.

• Ink Business Preferred Credit Card: You will receive primary rental coverage against collision damage and theft when renting a car for business purposes, up to the car's actual cash value, when you decline the rental company's insurance and charge the rental to your card. This applies to the majority of rental cars in the U.S. and overseas.

• Capital One Venture X Rewards Credit Card: This card offers primary rental coverage against theft and accident damage up to the real cash value of the vehicle (up to $75,000) if you choose to charge the rental to your card instead of the insurance provided by the rental company.

Invest in security

There are a few disadvantages even though ordering items from the convenience of your home is convenient. For starters, an item might be delivered broken or, worse still, pilfered.

On the other hand, purchase protection is typically included with credit cards and provides replacement coverage for lost or stolen goods. Just be aware that there is typically a cap on the annual amount you can receive back or the number of items you can claim with this benefit.

The best credit cards with purchase protection that we suggest are listed below:

• Chase Freedom Flex: up to 120 days after purchase, up to $500 per claim and $50,000 per account, protected against theft or damage.

• Chase Freedom Unlimited: up to 120 days following purchase, protection against loss or theft; $500 maximum per claim and $50,000 maximum per account.

• American Express Blue Cash Preferred Card: Maximum claim amount of $1,000 per covered purchase and $50,000 per covered card annually; purchase protection for up to 90 days from the date of purchase.

Warranty prolongations

Large-ticket purchases, like computers and televisions, typically come with warranties that cover any issues you may run across for a predetermined amount of time.

However, what happens if your brand-new computer breaks down a few days after the guarantee ends? That's where the extended warranty feature on a credit card can help.

Extending the manufacturer's warranty period by a predetermined amount of time—typically a year, but occasionally longer—is a perk that many rewards credit cards offer. Similar to a manufacturer's guarantee, this extended warranty will normally pay for the cost of replacing or repairing an item (up to the original purchase price).

My selections for the top credit cards with extended warranty protection are as follows:

• American Express Gold Card: For qualifying warranties of five years or less, the original manufacturer's warranty is extended by up to one year, with a $10,000 maximum coverage amount for each item (up to $50,000 per eligible card for each year).

• Chase Freedom Unlimited: Up to $50,000 per account, this benefit extends eligible U.S. manufacturer's warranties, which are three years or less, by one year, with a $10,000 maximum coverage amount per claim.

Mobile phone safety

Many of us consider our cell phones to be lifelines because they allow us to access the Internet primarily and stay in touch with friends and family.

If your cell phone is damaged, your credit card could be able to assist. Cell phone protection is a feature of certain credit cards that usually protects your phone in case it is lost, stolen, or destroyed. Usually, you have to pay your monthly phone bill with your credit card to profit from this offer. Additionally, the total number of claims you can file in a year and the amount of each claim are typically capped.

These are a few best choices for credit cards that safeguard cell phones:

• Ink Business Preferred Credit Card: Up to $1,000 in cell phone protection against covered theft or damage is available to cardholders and employees listed on the monthly mobile bill paid with this card; there is a $100 deductible for the first three claims made per calendar year.

• Wells Fargo Active Cash Card: When you pay your phone bill with your card each month, you can receive protection against theft or damage up to $600 per claim (with a $25 deductible); you can only file two claims annually.

• Chase Freedom Flex: You can receive up to $800 in damage or theft coverage per claim and $1,000 in annual coverage when you pay your phone bill with your card. You can file up to two claims annually; there is a $50 deductible.

To sum up

Credit cards are useful instruments for more than just making purchases and accumulating points. Spend some time learning more about the advantages that each credit card offers when searching for the greatest ones. Although a card's large welcome bonus could entice you, it might also include some fantastic but little-known benefits and protections.

The Burden of Student Loans

According to the Education Data Initiative, approximately 43 million Americans have student loan debt totaling $1.7 trillion, which is roughly half of the yearly revenue of the United States government.

As students spend decades repaying loans rather than purchasing homes, autos, and other necessities, this $1.7 trillion might be reinvested directly into our economy.

Tuition and student loan debt are at current high levels because higher education will always be in high demand, not because they have to be.

According to Forbes, the average cost of tuition, fees, room, and board has increased 180 percent since 1980, adjusted for inflation; in 1980, the average student graduated with a debt of $12,831; that amount is expected to rise to $31,100 in 2021.

Many opponents of the new policy argue that canceling the loans of everyone who still owes the debt is not fair to those who have already paid their obligations; it is unfair that they had to take out those loans and pay them back in the first place, but that is not a justification not to cancel the debt.

The fact that earlier generations had to endure this burden does not suggest that future generations should as well.

Furthermore, rising interest rates aggravate student loan debt. Federal student loans for undergraduates have an interest rate of 4.99 percent, according to Bankrate. While this figure may not appear spectacular, it is about $1,500 less than the typical student loan borrower's debt of $28,950.

The interest rate on federal loans is 4.99% however private loans can have interest rates as high as 13%.

These percentages build up over time, and students end up paying far more than they were originally lent.

Students should not be penalized for attempting to continue their education; burdening students with tens of thousands, if not hundreds of thousands, of dollars in debt simply for attempting to create a good foundation for their careers is clearly unethical.

This is a big issue that affects many University of Iowa students' lives; according to the Des Moines Register, UI students who took out loans graduated with an average of $26,200 for locals and roughly $34,880 for nonresidents.

The Biden administration should execute the plan offered by Sen. Bernie Sanders during his 2020 presidential campaign, which includes a 0.5 percent tax on stock trading, a 0.1 percent fee on bond trades, and a 0.005 percent cost on derivative trades to pay for the cancellation of all debt.

These tiny taxes will generate more than $2 trillion in revenue over the next ten years, more than enough to satisfy the whole national student debt.

Finally, student loan debt is a severe, unneeded challenge imposed on millions of Americans for the sole purpose of corporate profits, and the only way to correct this is to eliminate all student loan debt.

Five debt-reduction strategies

Getting out of debt may appear to be an impossible undertaking; you may be overwhelmed or intimidated by the amount of debt you have, and you may be unsure where to begin. Here are five steps to get you started on your debt-free journey:

STEP 1

Make a plan. Every effective endeavor starts with a well-defined goal. You may wish to get rid of all of your debts, or you may want to get rid of only one. Just keep in mind to make your aim SMART. To help you stay focused, write it down and post it somewhere you will see it every day.

STEP 2

Make a list of your present obligations. To get out of debt, you must have an exact and thorough list of your bills.

You may need to obtain copies of all three of your credit reports from Equifax, Experian, and TransUnion. This should provide you with information on current debts, including any bills that are in collections or judgments.

Your credit reports may also contain information about your most current reported amounts, loan terms, and creditor contact information.

You may, however, have debts that are not listed on your credit reports, such as:

• Loans from family or friends

• Payday loans, financial institutions, and pawn businesses

• Loans from persons or businesses that do not report to Equifax, Experian, or TransUnion

Also, provide this information.

STEP 3

Learn about your state's statute of limitations, which governs the amount of time a creditor has to recover a debt legally.

This is especially critical if you have debts that are being collected. Do not cease paying a debt because the statute of limitations is approaching or has passed. You should get legal counsel on how to manage debts that are approaching or have passed the statute of limitations.

Use the information you've gathered to prioritize debt payments if necessary. In general, secured debt takes precedence over unsecured debt because secured debt is backed by an asset.

- Your place of residence

- Your Vehicle

- Household appliances

- Any purchase made with a home equity line of credit

When you owe money for state or federal taxes, federal student loans, child support, and/or alimony, your accounts or wages can be garnished at a higher rate or without court proceedings, and a lien can be placed on your property in some cases, so these debts are often a higher priority than commercial debts.

Does this imply that you can avoid making credit card or medical debt payments? The answer is "no." Missing any debt payment can have serious implications; nevertheless, it is critical to understand how serious those consequences are. If you do not have enough money to pay off all of your debts, you may have to make difficult decisions; nevertheless, make certain that you understand the risks and repercussions of those actions.

STEP 4

Create a plan. There are two general debt reduction or eradication plans or approaches:

• The "avalanche" strategy is also known as the "high-interest rate method." This method involves listing your loans from greatest to lowest interest rate. You have completed all of your regular payments. You allocate any money left over in your budget to the debt with the greatest interest rate. The goal is to reduce or eliminate this debt as soon as possible because it is the most expensive. After you have paid off this loan, you repeat the process with the debt with the lowest interest rate.

• Low Balance Method: Also referred to as the "snowball" method. This method involves listing your debts from the lowest total balance to the greatest total balance. You have completed all of your regular payments. You allocate any money left over in your budget to the debt with the lowest balance. The goal is to pay down or erase this debt as soon as possible. After you have paid off this obligation, you continue the process by applying any additional funds to the debt with the next lowest balance.

STEP 5

Maintain your strategy. Each month, you will come closer to your objective of debt reduction or elimination. Setbacks are common; the important thing is to get back on track.

If you require assistance, seek it. Share your accomplishments and problems with trustworthy friends or family members, a counselor, or even on social media.

You can also get help from a consumer credit counseling agency in your town or region. These are charitable organizations that are members of the National Foundation for Credit Counseling.

These counselors will help you create a plan and may even propose a Debt Management Plan. A Debt Management Plan is a payment schedule that will assist you in repaying your obligations.

Chapter 2

Outsmart the banks

Assume you want to buy a pair of $100 pants, and the angel and devil appear on your right and left shoulders, representing the bank and your financial guardian, who wants to fight the banks.

You explain to both shoulders that you want to buy this pair of $100 pants, and the devil approves, saying that you need these jeans; they'll make you look fantastic and will complete your wardrobe once and for all, and you can put them on your credit card and worry about it later.

The angel then asks, "Do you know what $100 will be worth in 40 years if invested responsibly?" You answer, "Maybe $200?" The angel shakes its head and says, "$1,082.85." Yes, $100 can be worth $1082.85 in 40 years if invested responsibly at 6% compounded quarterly.

They claim that if the United States wealth was spread fairly, every citizen on the planet would receive $700,000

This is a fantastic notion, but it will only be realized if everyone makes better shopping decisions. The key to accumulating money is not spending it, and to be honest, most people are shortsighted when it comes to saving.

What to AVOID Buying

Every day should start with breakfast, and it should start at home. Rather than paying $5 for a coffee at Starbucks, invest in a $400 cappuccino machine; if you get a cappuccino every day, this equipment will begin saving you money within 15 weeks.

If you change your breakfast and lunch habits, you can easily save $20 each day, which adds up to more than $5,000 per year if only work days are included.

Examine your monthly costs and discover where your money goes. Your initial goal should be to spend less than you earn; if you've accomplished that, try to reduce it by 18% and put that money into savings. This is the number one step towards bankruptcy.

Never keep money in your checking account.

It's a little more complicated than that, but when you put money in your bank account, the bank will lend it to other individuals in the form of a mortgage, giving you little to no interest and even charging you to store your money.

A mix of equities (stocks), bonds, and mutual funds is usually adequate; if you're unfamiliar with the stock market, stick to mutual funds or read a book. If your employer provides a 401(k), you should contribute the maximum amount that they will match.

Open an IRA or Roth IRA if your employer does not provide benefits; these are basic steps that everyone should take to save for retirement. Get a second job if you don't have enough money right now. There are numerous reasons why you cannot save right now. If you believe their justifications, the bank will ALWAYS win.

Even if you can only invest $100 per month at 6% compounded semi-annually, you'll have more than $200,000 in 40 years; do the same with $500 per month, and you'll be just shy of a million dollars.

Bottom line: Don't leave your money sitting in your bank account; instead, invest it with a professional financial advisor who can help you achieve your investment goals, and don't put it off until next month or year; the key to developing wealth is for it to compound over time.

Credit cards exist solely to allow you to accumulate points.

Banks invented winning; some may have lost recently (2008), but it was a drop in the bucket in the history of banks.

According to Value Penguin, 38% of American households have credit card debt (also known as revolving debt), with a grand total of just under a trillion dollars as of 3/2016, meaning that banks earn more than a billion dollars each month on credit card interest.

You have two options if you do not want to be a statistic:

A- Don't play the game; instead, after you've paid off your credit cards, cut them up; you won't win, but you won't be a part of the problem.

B- Leverage the bank: To start collecting points, pay off your credit card before the conclusion of your monthly cycle.

Stop buying unneeded products and pay off your credit cards as quickly as possible because interest is compounded by the second. When you pay the minimum balance, the majority of your payment is used to interest. If you select option a, pay them off and contact your bank to close your account.

You have a chance to beat the banks at their own game if you choose B. Check the terms of your credit card, as many do not begin charging interest until charges are carried over to the next billing cycle. When is that going to happen? Your credit card will show "minimum balance due by MM/DD/YY." Forget the minimum and pay the entire debt by that date.

Even if your account is empty, you can earn incentives.

If you are responsible and pay off your card before the end of the payment cycle, you should look into different rewards credit cards that offer 1% cashback on everything you buy or even more.

You will be in a good position to win if you only use your rewards credit card for necessities like food, water, phone, and utilities. Assume your household spends $15,000 on these products per year. Banks will pay you $150 in cash back if your rewards card offers 1% cash back. This may not appear to be a large sum, but you moved from paying the banks to them paying you. That's a win in my book!

Remember that the "cash back" ploy is a marketing ploy designed to prey on the inexperienced; don't sign up for a rewards card unless you can consistently pay off your debt on time for a few months in a row.

Buying a House

Purchasing a home is thrilling, but what you can afford is a somewhat ambiguous term. What you should be asked is, "How much do you want to spend per month?" After that, think about how much interest you want to pay the bank throughout the life of the loan.

I'll explain using my own personal experience. When we originally started shopping for houses, we had a maximum budget of $350,000.

Then we discovered an incredible fixer-upper in an incredible neighborhood for nearly $100,000 cheaper. If we purchased our maximum-budget home, we would need a 30-year mortgage to make the payments and would pay a higher interest rate.

A 15-year mortgage has higher total monthly payments, but you will pay less interest. Why? Banks view time (length) as a negative risk element, and if your loan has a longer tenure, the bank will want compensation for the added risk. The bank will win by a mere 1% difference, which may potentially amount to $100,000 more out of pocket over the life of your loan.

This is why, when considering how much you can "afford" each month, buying a less expensive home with a shorter-term mortgage is a better alternative.

Consider getting a shorter-term loan.

We also saved for a few years and came up with a 20% down payment to avoid paying PMI, which is normally 5%, reducing 1.5% from our loan rates. If the angel and the devil appeared again on my shoulders, the devil would shrug and say, "Who argues over 1.5%?"

The angel would then raise his hand and declare, "I do." If you buy a $250,000 home at 3.36% interest for 15 years, you will pay approximately $307,000. At 4.86% interest, the identical $250,000 property will cost you $458,000.

This is not to say that you should burden yourself with extravagant payments; each circumstance is different, but consider postponing the ideal house in favor of a house that can become a dream house until you can afford the dream house.

Many people begin a diet with a fitness goal in mind, such as "losing twenty pounds." I'm sure many people achieve that goal, but what happens next? Return to your old diet? The best diet goal is to permanently alter your food and life patterns.

Outwit the banks to save money.

Beating the banks, or, let's face it, saving money, is the same thing: if you establish a goal for how much money you want to save and merely change your spending habits for that time frame, you will revert to your former self once you achieve it.

Choosing the right bank is also important; seek one that offers attractive bonuses, competitive interest rates, and other options to help you maximize your savings, such as Citibank.

Saving money and amassing a fortune is a way of life for many wealthy entrepreneurs. This is because they got to where they are via hard work and will not risk being pushed back to the beginning.

It's time to commit to making better financial decisions if you're reading this. Determine what you can eliminate and then calculate how much money you will save each month as a result. Set up a monthly auto-transfer from your bank account to your investment account to beat the banks and get the benefits.

Establishing no-fee high-interest accounts

What to Know About High-Yield Savings Accounts

What is a high-yielding savings account, exactly?

High-yield savings accounts often give a substantially greater annual percentage yield (APY) than ordinary savings accounts, allowing depositors to earn more while still enjoying the security of a federally insured account. Traditional savings accounts are typically available in brick-and-mortar banks and larger banks, and they can earn almost nothing, often around 0.01 percent APY.

Consumers looking for a guaranteed yield should investigate a certificate of deposit (CD), and a no-penalty CD may be a viable alternative for those who want a fixed APY as well as the ability to withdraw funds without penalty.

Savings accounts often generate compound interest, which simply means that you will receive interest on interest on both your principal and the interest that accumulates over time.

To comprehend high-yield savings terms

Consider the following characteristics while shopping for a high-yield savings account. Consider Bankrate's expert assessments of significant banks, many of which offer high-interest savings accounts, when determining which account is best for you.

Annual percentage yield is abbreviated as APY.

The effect of compounding, which is just the interest you receive on interest, is combined in APY. You will receive interest on your initial deposit as well as the interest that accumulates over time.

High-yield savings accounts are a safe location to earn interest on your money as long as the assets are federally insured. The FDIC guarantees up to $250,000 per depositor, per FDIC-insured bank, and per ownership category, while the NCUA guarantees up to $250,000 per share owner, per insured credit union, and per account ownership category.

This federal insurance ensures that consumers' funds are protected in the case of a bank failure, as long as they stay within the limitations and restrictions.

You can use the FDIC's Bank Find Suite to see if your bank is FDIC-insured. If you bank with a credit union, make sure it is insured by the NCUA.

Who should open an online high-yield savings account?

High-yield savings accounts with no minimum opening deposit, no minimum balance requirement and no monthly service fees are a good choice for practically everyone since they can help people with a range of financial goals and at different stages of their financial lives.

The advantages and disadvantages of online high-yield savings accounts

Savings accounts are a fantastic place to save money for a number of financial goals; here are the benefits and drawbacks of online high-yield savings accounts to help you determine which one is best for you.

Pros

• Online high-yield savings accounts frequently offer a higher annual percentage yield (APY) than traditional savings accounts.

• Many high-yield savings accounts have digital tools that allow you to manage your money from a computer, smartphone, or tablet.

• The federal government insures high-yield savings accounts at most banks and credit unions, ensuring the safety of your funds.

• Unlike certificates of deposit, funds in a high-yield savings account are available immediately.

Cons

• The rates on high-yield savings accounts fluctuate and may fall.

• Some banks limit monthly withdrawals and transfers to six.

• Savings accounts are not often utilized to write cheques.

• Investing your money could lead to more returns.

• Not all online banks offer branch or ATM access.

Establishing a High-Yield Savings Account

You should select the greatest bank and account for you. The perfect account for you must meet the minimum deposit requirement, and if it has a minimum balance requirement, you must maintain a level above it to avoid a monthly service fee.

You'll want to earn a competitive interest rate on your high-yield savings, which may preclude you from using a local bank because FDIC-insured internet banks often offer the highest returns.

Here's how a high-yield savings account is done, straightforward to open:

1. Look around. Online banks, traditional banks with branches, and credit unions all offer high-yield savings accounts. Because online banks don't have the overhead involved with maintaining branches, they can pass on the savings to consumers in the form of higher interest rates. Compare fees, services, and APY to determine the best fit for your financial situation.

2. Complete an application. After deciding on a high-interest savings account, you must complete an application, either online or in person.

Personal information such as your driver's license number, Social Security number, mailing address, and date of birth will be requested by the bank or credit union. You may be required to scan a copy of a government-issued photo ID while applying online. You may also need to remove any security freezes on your credit file.

3. Make a deposit into your account. If your chosen bank requires an opening deposit, you can make one online by linking a checking account to the new savings account and transferring funds. You may be able to fund the new savings account via wire transfer or by mailing a cheque, depending on the bank. A mobile check deposit is another possibility.

If you fail to fulfill the account's minimum deposit requirement, you may be charged a maintenance fee or get a lower-than-expected interest rate until the minimum is met.

Alternatives to high-yield savings accounts

Traditional savings vs. high-yield savings accounts

There are some parallels between high-yield savings accounts and ordinary savings accounts, but there are some significant differences.

High-yield accounts, for example, are frequently available online, although other classic savings accounts, such as passbook and statement savings accounts, may be limited to opening and managing at a bank branch. As the name implies, high-yield savings accounts often earn substantially greater rates than ordinary savings accounts, and they may require a bigger beginning deposit and a minimum monthly balance requirement. Depending on the institution, both accounts are subject to monthly fees however many banks provide no-fee, high-yield, and standard savings accounts.

CD vs. high-yield savings account

A high-yield savings account is a liquid account for money that you might need to withdraw at any time. You can deposit money into this account at any time, in addition to making withdrawals on demand (albeit they may be limited each statement cycle).

CDs, unlike savings accounts, lock in your money for a set period of time, and if you withdraw it before the term is up, you'll usually be charged an early withdrawal penalty, and you can't usually add money to a regular CD while it's still open.

High-yield savings account vs. money market account

In general, a high-yield savings account does not enable users to write checks against the account, but many money market accounts do.

Savings accounts are far more common than money market accounts however, many institutions provide both.

High-interest savings account versus. Savings account

Savings accounts may have a limit on the number of withdrawals or transfers you can make in a single statement cycle, but checking accounts do not.

Checking accounts are used for transactional operations like paying bills or using debit cards, and they frequently have no monthly transaction restrictions.

Chapter 3

Prepare to make an investment.

What is the definition of investing?

We invest consistently throughout our lives, whether consciously or unconsciously, whether it's our time gaining a university degree or our energy learning to prepare a new recipe. We frequently undertake these things because we expect them to be valuable in the future, such as earning that ideal job after graduating from university. Profit from financial investments is sometimes referred to as an investment return, and it is expressed as a percentage. For example, if you invest €1000 and receive €1000 back at the conclusion of the investment period, your profit is €100, representing a 10% investment return.

What makes people want to invest?

People have utilized investment to gain riches for hundreds of years. Long-term investing is beneficial because investment returns compound (become greater and bigger) with each reinvested, allowing you to accomplish your financial goals faster.

For example, if you invest €100 every month at an 8% interest rate for the next 20 years, your savings will grow at a quicker pace each year. This gives many people the financial resources to pay for school, mortgages, automobiles, trips, retirement, and so on. As a result, people commonly turn to investment for opportunities.

Saving vs. Investing

Saving is concerned with saving money so that it is available when needed. For example, if you save €50 every week for the following five years, you will have those funds at the end of that time. Saving normally yields no returns because there is no risk involved (even with interest-bearing savings accounts, returns might be negative owing to inflation).

You can expect a return on your investment, but there's a chance you won't get your money back or make any profit; this uncertainty, however, can be addressed through investment methods.

Because your reward (return) as an investor is frequently predicated on the level of risk of an investment - something known as the risk and return trade-off the higher the risk in an investment, the greater the possible return.

The terms investing and trading are commonly used interchangeably, although they are not the same thing. At a high level, investing focuses on achieving long-term investment returns; many people already participate in this form of investing through government-sponsored retirement plans. Trading, on the other hand, concentrates on short-term gains by buying and selling investments on a regular basis.

Who is the typical investor?

Every year, private (individual) and institutional (businesses or organizations) investors invest trillions of Euros in Europe. Over 50 million private investors from 21 million families invest their money in Germany alone. France, the Netherlands, Italy, and Luxembourg are among the countries having a substantial number of private investors.

What do the majority of people invest in?

You hold an asset when you own anything of worth that can be turned into money. Assets might be liquid, which means they can be converted to money fast, or illiquid, which means it takes longer and is more complicated. Asset classes, which are groups of assets with similar characteristics, are used in the investment market to classify assets.

Stocks

A stock, also known as equities or shares, is a unit of ownership in a firm or corporation. Companies offer their stock to the public on stock exchanges, which allow buyers and sellers to trade equities. The first stock exchange, the Amsterdam Stock Exchange, opened in the early 1600s, making this one of the world's oldest forms of investment.

Some stock investments give out dividends, which are a percentage of a company's profits, to investors, whilst others are purchased and held in the expectation of increasing in value over time.

Despite being a dangerous asset class, stocks are regularly discussed in the media and are one of the most discussed asset groups.

Bonds

Bonds are debt-based investments; when an investor buys a bond, they are basically lending their money to a government or corporation to support their financial needs. When you purchase a bond, you will receive fixed repayments of your investment plus interest, providing you with a return on your initial investment.

Government bonds and corporate bonds are the two primary forms of bonds, and both are graded based on how hazardous the borrower is, for example, the possibility of them not repaying you. Bonds with high ratings are known as investment-grade bonds, whereas bonds with lower ratings are known as high-yield bonds. Investment-grade bonds often provide minimal returns yet, their low risk appeals to many investors, particularly those who are risk-averse.

Real estate investing

We are all familiar with real estate; it is the homes we live in, the stores we frequent, and the offices from which we work. Despite being considered dangerous, real estate investments are one of the most prevalent (and expensive) asset classes in the financial world. It is popular among institutions with multi-billion dollar real estate funds, in addition to private investors.

Commodities

Commodities also represent items that we come into contact with on a daily basis. A commodity is a tradable (physical) good, such as raw resources or agricultural products. Sugar, gold, oil, and wheat are common examples. To be considered a commodity, anything must be produced or sold in a similar quality by a large number of people/companies.

bank account or any savings in a fixed-term deposit.

Cash is a low-risk asset type since it is immediately available when investors need it, even if it is in the form of a short-term fixed-term deposit.

Where Should You Start If You Want to Start Investing?

Investing methods come in a variety of shapes and sizes, and how people choose to invest is heavily influenced by their prior experience and financial aspirations. Despite the fact that the investment landscape appears to be vast, there are options for everyone.

Setting investment goals is a great place to start; once you've established your goals and budget, you can begin investigating which assets or asset classes best meet your financial objectives and risk tolerance.

Investment platforms that provide easy, automated investment techniques can be a smart place to start because they are developed with professional analysis and data, eliminating the need for prior experience or timely in-depth study.

The roadmap to constructing wealth

Investments in exchange-traded funds (huge investment portfolios in which investors can acquire shares) are also quite straightforward because they are handled by investment firms and do not necessitate any labor on the part of the investor.

Some investors have only one asset, such as a real estate investment, but others have a variety of assets, establishing an investment portfolio. It is critical not to put all of your eggs in one basket when developing a portfolio. Diversification is an investment technique that involves spreading modest amounts of money across numerous assets so that your lower-risk investments balance out your higher-risk ones.

Choose assets based on your risk tolerance.

Trying to figure out how to invest money means wondering where you should place your money, and the answer will depend on your goals and willingness to take on greater risk in exchange for higher potential investment returns.

• Stocks: Individual shares (a stake in a corporation) in which you believe the value will rise; learn more about stocks.

• Bonds: Bonds allow a firm or government to borrow money from you in order to fund a project or restructure other debt. Bonds are fixed-income investments that typically pay monthly interest to investors before returning the principal on a predetermined maturity date.

• Mutual funds: Investing in funds, such as mutual funds, index funds, or exchange-traded funds (ETFs), enables you to purchase a large number of stocks, bonds, or other investments all at once. Mutual funds provide quick diversification by combining investor funds and investing them in a portfolio of investments that fit with the fund's stated aim. Funds can be actively managed, with investments chosen by a professional manager, or they can track an index.

• Real estate: Buying a home or becoming a landlord isn't the only way to diversify your investment portfolio beyond the traditional mix of stocks and bonds; you can also invest in real estate investment trusts (REITs), which are similar to mutual funds for real estate, or through online real estate investing platforms, which pool investor money.

You may want to invest in stocks or stock funds if you have a high-risk tolerance, a long time horizon, and can stomach volatility; if you have a low-risk tolerance, you may want to invest in bonds, which are more stable and less volatile.

Your aims are also important when creating your portfolio; for long-term objectives, your portfolio can be more aggressive and take more risks, perhaps resulting in higher returns. Therefore, you may want to buy more stocks than bonds.

Whatever course you choose, the best way to achieve your long-term financial goals while avoiding risk is to diversify your investments across asset classes.

This is referred to as asset diversification, and the proportion of money invested in each asset class is referred to as asset allocation. You should also diversify your investments within each asset type.

• Asset diversification means holding a varied portfolio of assets across industries, firm sizes, and geographic areas.

This is significant because different asset types — stocks, bonds, ETFs, mutual funds, and real estate — react differently to market conditions. When one goes up, another goes down. Choosing the correct balance will help your portfolio weather-changing markets and stay on track to meet your objectives.

• Asset allocation is the percentage of money invested in each asset type. For example, your asset allocation is 90/10 if you opt to invest 90% of your money in stocks and 10% in bonds, depending on your risk tolerance, time horizon, and goals. You should diversify your stock portfolio by investing 90% of your money in large-cap companies, mid-cap stocks, international equities, and value stocks.

Creating a varied portfolio of individual investments

Having a savings account is not enough.

Saving money is important, but it is only half the issue. Smart savers start by building a sufficient emergency fund. However, after three to six months of saving in a savings account or investing in a money market account, investing in the financial markets offers a plethora of potential benefits.

The level of compounding.

Compounding occurs when an investment generates earnings or dividends that are then reinvested and generate earnings of their own; in other words, compounding occurs when your investments generate earnings from earlier earnings.

When you purchase a dividend-paying stock,

For example, you could consider reinvesting dividends to capitalize on the potential power of compounding.

Start investing as soon as possible and reinvest your dividends and other payments automatically to help optimize the potential benefits of compounding.

Risk-return trade-off

Different investments provide varying degrees of potential return and market risk.

The probability that an investment will generate a lower-than-expected return or lose value is referred to as risk.

The amount of money earned on assets invested, or the overall increase in the value of the investment, is referred to as return.

Investing in stocks

Have the potential for bigger profits, whereas investing in a money market or savings account is unlikely to have the same return potential but is considered less risky than investing in stocks.

Your appetite or tolerance for risk determines the amount of risk you carry. Only you know how much risk you're ready to take in exchange for the chance of better profits.

However, if you want to outperform inflation, you may need to take some risks.

Chapter 4

Making a financial plan

What is the definition of a budget?

A budget is a written plan that details how much money you want to spend each month.

Without a budget, you risk running out of money before your next paycheck.

A budget illustrates:

• How much money you make

• Your spending habits

Why do I need a budget?

A budget can help you make the following decisions:

• How much money you should spend

• If you can save money on some items while spending more on others.

For example, if your budget reveals that you spend $100 per month on clothing, you may choose to spend only $50 on clothing and use the rest of your money to pay bills or save for something else.

Why should I save money?

Saving money can be challenging, especially when your expenses rise but your income does not. Here are some reasons why you should try to save money even if it is difficult.

• Emergencies - Small quantities of money saved now may come in handy later; everyone has unexpected bills.

• Expensive items - We occasionally have to pay for expensive items such as a car, a trip, or a security deposit on an apartment; if you have the money to pay for such expensive items, you will have more possibilities.

• Your goals - You may want to pay for college classes or visit family in another country.

You can plan ahead of time and save money to avoid having to use a credit card or borrow money to pay for these goals.

A well-structured budget may help you see where your money is coming from, where it is going, and how much you can save or invest, which is essential for managing personal finances, saving money, and reaching financial objectives.

Guide to creating a budget

1. Set Specific Financial Goals: Before you begin, decide what you want to accomplish. Is it for debt repayment? an installment payment on a house? Establish an emergency fund. Knowing your objectives will motivate you to stick to your budget.

2. Gather Financial Information: Compile all sources of income and monthly spending, separating fixed costs (such as rent or mortgage payments) from variable costs (such as dining out or entertainment).

3. Maintain and categorize your expenses:

- Fixed Expenses: These are monthly expenses that do not change, such as rent, mortgage, car payments, and insurance.

- Variable Expenses: These are expenses that are subject to change, such as groceries, dining out, entertainment, and gasoline.

- Periodic Expenses: Costs that occur on a quarterly or annual basis but must be budgeted for, such as annual subscriptions or quarterly insurance premiums.

4. Create a Budget:

- Zero-Based Budget: Each dollar has a purpose; total revenue minus total costs should equal zero; this does not mean that you spend all of your money but that each dollar is assigned to a category, such as savings or debt payments.

- The 50/30/20 Rule states that you should set aside 50% of your income for essentials, 30% for wants, and 20% for savings or debt reduction.

Cash Envelope System: Put money in different envelopes for different spending categories, and when the money is gone, that's the limit for that category for the month.

5. As the month progresses, check for areas where you may be overspending or under-budgeting and make appropriate modifications.

6. Follow Your Budget: Even the best-planned budget is useless if it is not followed; keep your goals in mind and be vigilant.

7. At least once a month, go over your budget to evaluate if you stayed within your budgetary restrictions and where you may improve.

8. Plan for Emergencies: Always budget for unplanned expenses and have 3-6 months' worth of living expenses in a savings account that is easily accessible.

9. Use apps: Budgeting software and apps like YNAB (You Need a Budget), Mint, and Every Dollar can connect to your bank accounts and categorize and track your spending for you.

10. Reduce Debt: If you have debt, especially high-interest debt like credit card debt, devise a plan to pay it off as soon as possible, either by prioritizing bills based on interest rate or by employing tactics like the "debt snowball" (paying off the smallest debts first).

11. Start saving and investing for long-term goals such as retirement once you have a handle on your spending and an emergency fund.

Remember that the purpose of a budget is to give you freedom, not to limit it; by understanding where your money is going, you'll be able to make better decisions and reach your financial goals.

The contrast between cheap folks and conscious spenders

The distinction between "cheap people" and "conscious spenders" is based on their values, aspirations, and motivations for spending (or not spending). While both may attempt to spend less than necessary, their reasons and methods differ.

1. Inspiration:

- Cheap People: Their main purpose is to spend as little money as possible, often regardless of value, and the act of saving money is usually the main reason.

- Conscious Spenders: They value over cost, and their motivation is to spend money wisely and make every dollar matter, usually in accordance with a wider set of values or goals.

2. Cost versus value:

- Cheap People: Are more likely to value price over quality and may buy an item merely because it is the cheapest option, even if it is of low quality.

- Conscious Spenders: Think about the long-term worth of a purchase; they may spend more on a high-quality item that will last longer because they believe it is a better investment.

3. Relationship with Money:

- Cheap People: Have a scarcity mindset, believing they will never have enough and must continually hoard and save.

- Conscious Spenders: Have an abundance or balanced mindset, appreciate the importance of saving but, also believe in spending when it aligns with their principles.

4. Decision-Making Process:

- Cheap People: Price has a large influence on spending decisions.

- Conscious Spenders: Decisions are influenced by a number of factors, including the item's value, environmental impact, necessity, and alignment with personal goals or beliefs.

5. Interactions with Others:

- Cheap People: They may refuse to contribute their fair share, underspend when it is their turn to treat someone or be too concerned with money in social circumstances.

- Conscious Spenders: are fair in their financial interactions with others and avoid putting relationships in jeopardy for the sake of money.

6. Priorities and objectives:

- Cheap People: The main goal is to save money, even if it means foregoing other aspects of life.

- Conscious Spenders: Have larger goals such as financial independence, ethical business support, environmental impact reduction, or ensuring quality of life.

7. Adaptability:

- Cheap People: Have rigorous spending habits, avoiding expenditures even when they are necessary or essential.

- Conscious Spenders: They are adaptable and change their spending habits in response to their circumstances, needs, and long-term goals.

Unexpected Costs Management

Unexpected expenses, which can arise from a range of situations such as medical emergencies, unanticipated car repairs, or necessary property maintenance, are a common source of concern in personal finance. Here's a step-by-step technique for dealing with similar situations:

1. Keep Calm: The first step is to deal with the situation calmly; take a deep breath, assess the situation, and ascertain the exact nature and urgency of the expense.

2. Determine the Price:

- Determine the overall cost.

- Determine whether the matter is actually urgent or if it can be postponed.

- Look for cheaper alternatives or solutions.

3. Examine Your Emergency Fund: Ideally, you should have an emergency fund set up to handle unforeseen bills, which should comprise 3-6 months of living expenses. Make sure you have one, then use it.

4. Reorganize Your Budget:

-review your monthly budget

- Determine whether any discretionary expenditure (such as entertainment, dining out, etc.) may be cut to cover the unexpected cost.

- If the expense is significant, you may need to adjust your budget for several months.

5. If you don't have an emergency fund, or if it's insufficient, consider tapping into other resources; it's not deal, but it's better than collecting high-interest debt.

6. Sell unwanted stuff: If you have stuff lying around that you don't need, consider selling it on platforms like eBay, Craigslist, or Facebook Marketplace to earn money.

7. Avoid High-Interest Debt: While credit cards and payday loans may be enticing, try to avoid them because they typically have high-interest rates. If you must use a credit card, search for one with a 0% introductory APR and intend to pay it off before interest accrues.

8. Payment Plans and Negotiations: If you have an unexpected bill, try to negotiate a lower price or set up a payment plan to spread the cost over time.

9. Seek Assistance: Depending on the nature of the expenditure, you may need to:

- Look into community aid programs.

- Check to see if any charities or organizations can help you.

10. Consider the following techniques for growing your revenue in the short term:

- Working as a contractor

- Working part-time

- Gig economy jobs, such as ridesharing or food delivery.

11. Examine and Research:

- After the crisis has passed, reflect on what occurred and whether it might have been expected.

-make sure to learn from the circumstance.

Chapter 5

Saving when sleeping

Psychological Techniques for Saving Money

Using psychological techniques can have a significant impact on your spending patterns and assist you in saving more money. Here are some ways and principles from psychology that you might apply:

1. Set explicit, measurable goals: Visualizing exact, measurable goals (such as saving for a vacation, buying a home, or generating an emergency fund) can motivate you to save. Knowing the 'why' behind your efforts can be extremely motivating.

2. Paying using cash rather than credit cards can make spending more "painful" and palpable, and physically handing over money can make you more conscious of your expenditures.

3. Set up a percentage of your paycheck to go directly into savings as soon as you get paid; if it isn't in your bank account, you're less likely to spend it.

4. Use Envelopes: Put cash in envelopes for each category (e.g., groceries, entertainment), and when the cash is gone, that's your monthly limit. This method necessitates keeping track of your spending habits.

5. Avoid Instant pleasure: The "Marshmallow Test" shows that deferred pleasure can result in greater future rewards. If you're tempted to buy something impulsively, wait 24-48 hours to see if you still want it.

6. Loss Aversion: The misery of losing money is usually more intense than the delight of making money; to resist impulsive purchases, remind yourself of the suffering associated with unwise spending.

7. Visualize Savings Growth: Using charts or programs, track and visualize your savings growth; seeing progress can be motivating.

8. Limit Exposure: Unsubscribe from advertising emails and follow fewer brands on social media to reduce the temptation to make impulsive purchases.

9. Anchor Prices: Retailers frequently use the anchoring effect, in which a higher starting price (the "anchor") appears to make subsequent prices appear lower in contrast; be wary of this tactic and base pricing on genuine value and necessity.

10. Social Accountability: Share your financial goals with your friends and family; when others are aware of your intentions, you may feel more accountable.

11. Recognize when you're buying for emotional reasons and find other ways to cope, such as exercising or talking to a friend.

12. Downsize and declutter: Adopting a minimalist mindset can change your outlook on things, reducing your desire to acquire more.

13. Set milestones in your savings goals and give yourself small rewards as you meet them to make the process more fun.

14. Sunk Cost Fallacy: Don't let past financial mistakes affect your future spending; just because you've spent money on something in the past doesn't mean you have to continue doing so in the future.

Making your money to flow automatically.

1. Set up automated bill payments for your regular bills, such as rent/mortgage, utilities, and insurance, to ensure that these important expenses are paid on time and to avoid late fees or missing payments.

2. Set up automatic transfers to savings: Set up automatic transfers to your savings account every time you receive a paycheck to ensure that you are consistently saving and building your emergency fund or working toward other financial objectives.

3. Set up automatic retirement contributions from your paycheck: If your employer has a retirement plan, set up automatic contributions from your paycheck to ensure that you are saving for your future on a regular basis and taking advantage of any employer-matching incentives.

4. Consider automated investment platforms that can automatically invest a percentage of your savings in various portfolios, allowing you to build wealth over time without actively managing your assets.

5. Use budgeting applications or software that can automatically classify your expenses and generate spending reports so you may examine your spending and identify areas for improvement.

6. Set up automatic debt payments: If you have debt, such as credit card debt or student loans, set up automatic payments to ensure that you are continuously paying down your balances and avoiding late fees.

Chapter 6

Investing is not limited to the wealthy.

Completely correct! Investing is not only for the wealthy; everyone, regardless of income level, can start investing. Here are some of the reasons why investment is available to everyone:

1. Small investment amounts: You don't need a large sum of money to start investing; many investment platforms and brokerage firms allow you to begin with as little as $1, allowing you to start with whatever amount you're comfortable with and gradually increase your investments over time.

2. Diversification: Investing allows you to diversify your portfolio by spreading your investments across different assets, such as stocks, bonds, mutual funds, or real estate, which helps reduce risk. This can be done with small amounts of money by investing in low-cost index funds or exchange-traded funds (ETFs), which provide instant diversification.

3. Technology and automated investing: Robo-advisors and investment apps have made investing easier than ever before by using algorithms and automated processes to create and manage investment portfolios, making it accessible to people who may not have the time or knowledge to actively manage their investments.

4. Compound interest: Investing allows you to benefit from compound interest, which means your money can grow significantly over time.

5. Education and resources: There are numerous online and offline educational resources available to assist you in learning about investing and getting started, such as books, articles, podcasts, and videos; many brokerage firms also provide free instructional materials and resources to their clients.

Keep in mind that investing is a long-term game that necessitates patience and a well-defined investment strategy. Before making any investing decisions, it is also recommended that you consult with a financial advisor or undertake sufficient research.

Creating Your Own Portfolio: How to Select Investments

Choosing investments for your portfolio necessitates a combination of research, analysis, and a well-defined investing strategy; here are some starting points:

1. Clearly establish your investment objectives: Start by clearly outlining your investment objectives, taking into account factors such as your time horizon, risk tolerance, and financial ambitions. This can assist in guiding your investment decisions and ensure that you choose investments that are aligned with your objectives.

2. Investigate various investing options: Learn about numerous investment options such as stocks, bonds, mutual funds, ETFs, real estate, and commodities, as well as the characteristics, risks, and potential returns associated with each asset type.

3. Assess risk and return: Think about the risk-reward trade-off of each investment. Greater gains are frequently accompanied by greater risks.

Determine how much risk you are willing to accept and whether the potential profits of an investment match your risk tolerance.

4. Consider undertaking fundamental research when evaluating individual stocks or bonds, which comprises analyzing the company's financial health, management team, competitive advantage, industry trends, and future development potential. Examine financial records, annual reports, and news releases to learn about the company's performance and future.

5. Consider diversification: Spread your investments across many asset classes, industries, and geographies to lessen risk. This reduces the influence of a single investment or market event on your portfolio.

6. Monitor and review your assets' performance on a frequent basis; stay current on market trends and events that may affect your investments; and consider rebalancing your portfolio regularly to ensure that it remains aligned with your set goals.

7. Seek professional assistance if necessary: If you're unsure about picking investments on your own or need expert counsel, consider contacting a financial advisor who can make personalized recommendations based on your specific financial situation and goals.

Remember that investing contains risk, and there are no guarantees of returns; therefore, when constructing your investment portfolio, it is critical that you perform complete research, seek guidance if necessary, and make informed judgments.

Unbelievable cryptocurrency "investments"

Many investments that were considered "insane" or highly speculative at the time of their creation have turned out to be tremendously rewarding for early adopters in the context of Bitcoin. However, it is crucial to understand that the world of cryptocurrency investments is volatile, and previous performance is not a guarantee of future outcomes.

1. Bitcoin (BTC): When it was first introduced in 2009, it was worth fractions of a penny, and many people felt the concept of digital, decentralized money was ridiculous.

Now, it has reached levels in the tens of thousands of dollars per Bitcoin, resulting in spectacular profits for early investors.

2. Ethereum (ETH): The price of Ethereum's initial coin offering (ICO) in 2014 was around $0.30; by 2021, the price had climbed to more than $4,000. Ethereum pioneered the notion of smart contracts, which enabled the development of decentralized programs (DApps) on its platform.

3. Binance Coin (BNB): Originally developed as a utility token for the Binance cryptocurrency exchange, BNB has witnessed a significant value rise, particularly as Binance's ecosystem has expanded.

4. Dogecoin (DOGE): Initially thought to be a joke, Dogecoin surged in popularity and witnessed significant price increases, particularly in 2021.

5. Chain-link (LINK): Chain Link, an Oracle network that provides real-world data to smart contracts, was another project that witnessed tremendous growth.

6. Platforms such as Uniswap, Aave, and Compound, among others, have shown that decentralized lending, borrowing, and trading solutions are in significant demand.

7. Non-Fungible Tokens (NFTs): While the concept may have seemed unusual to some, numerous NFTs have sold for millions of dollars, and early developers and investors have reaped significant rewards.

These situations should be treated with caution taking into consideration the following:

- Volatility: Cryptocurrency prices can be extremely volatile, resulting in significant losses for many users.

- No Guarantee: Past performance is no guarantee of future results; just because a cryptocurrency has increased in value in the past does not mean that it will continue to rise in the future.

- Research: Before investing in any asset, including cryptocurrencies, thoroughly research the project, its utility, the team behind it, and its long-term viability.

- Regulation: The cryptocurrency industry is dealing with regulatory issues, which could affect the value and usability of individual tokens.

- Risk Management: To decrease risk, only invest what you can afford to lose, and diversify your investments.

While there have been profitable opportunities in the cryptocurrency realm, they must be approached with awareness and caution.

Chapter 7

How to Keep and Grow Your Financial System

Maintaining and expanding your money system requires consistent effort and good financial management; here are some techniques to help you accomplish your goal.

1. Budgeting: Create a budget to track your income and expenses, which will allow you to see where your money is going and make the necessary changes to save and invest.

2. Saving: Set up automatic transfers to a savings account and seek to consistently save a portion of your monthly salary to help you build an emergency fund and save for future goals.

3. To ease financial stress and free up funds for savings and investing, pay off high-interest debt first.

4. Invest wisely: Develop an investment strategy based on your risk tolerance and financial goals, educate yourself on various investment options, and consider diversifying your portfolio.

The roadmap to constructing wealth

5. Continue to study and grow by reading books, listening to podcasts, and attending webinars or workshops to increase your knowledge of personal finance and investment.

6. Re-balance your portfolio: On a regular basis, review your investment portfolio and appraise your holdings to verify that they are aligned with your goals and risk tolerance, and consider rebalancing your portfolio if necessary.

Set clear financial goals and divide them into smaller milestones to help you stay focused and motivated. Track your development on a regular basis and applaud your accomplishments.

8. Reduce unnecessary expenses: On a regular basis, evaluate your spending patterns and eliminate unnecessary or wasteful expenses, as well as reduce your lifestyle, if possible, to save more money.

9. Seek skilled counsel and assistance: To obtain specialized counsel and support, consider speaking with a financial advisor or planner who can assist you in making educated decisions and providing strategies tailored to your specific financial circumstances and goals.

10. Be patient and disciplined: It takes time to build and grow your money system. Maintain financial discipline and patience as you work toward your goals. Avoid making rash financial decisions and instead concentrate on long-term success.

Remember that everyone's financial journey is unique, so it's vital to analyze your personal financial situation, goals, and risk tolerance before implementing these measures. Adapt your financial system as needed to shifting circumstances and priorities.

Feed your money system-the more you put in, the more you get back.

When it comes to investing and growing your financial system, the adage "the more you put in, the more you will get" can be true. Here are some ideas for feeding your money system and maybe increasing your returns:

1. Improve your savings rate: The more money you can save and invest, the greater your chances of success. Look for ways to increase your income, reduce your consumption, and save more money for your assets.

2. Regularly contribute: Make it a habit to donate to your investments on a regular basis. Set up automatic transfers and make frequent donations, even if they are small because these consistent payments can compound and help your money grow over time.

3. Utilize business contributions: If your job offers a retirement savings plan, such as a 401(k) or pension plan, contribute enough to take full advantage of any employer matching contributions, which are basically free money and can significantly enhance your savings.

4. Consider side hustles, freelance work, rental income, or other investment ventures that can expand your financial resources and allow you to invest more.

5. Dividends and interest payments should be reinvested: If you hold stocks or bonds that produce dividends or interest, consider reinvesting those payments so that your money can compound and grow over time.

6. Improve your investment knowledge: Continue to educate yourself and improve your understanding of investing by remaining current on various investment techniques, asset classes, and market trends, which can help you make better investment decisions and potentially increase your profits.

7. Monitor and make changes to your portfolio: Review your investment portfolio on a regular basis and make changes as needed, keeping an eye on market conditions, economic trends, and investment performance. Rebalance your portfolio as needed to maintain the asset allocation you wanted.

It is critical to remember that investing involves risks, and there are no guarantees of returns; so, before making any investment decisions, evaluate your risk tolerance, consider diversification, and consult with a financial advisor.

The challenging component of managing your own portfolio

Managing your own portfolio can be challenging and time-consuming. Some of the more difficult aspects of managing your own portfolio are as follows:

1. Emotional biases: Managing your emotions is one of the most challenging challenges in investing. Emotions like fear and greed can impact decision-making and lead to impulsive conduct, so staying disciplined and avoiding emotional investment judgments is key.

2. Market volatility: Markets can be unpredictable and turbulent, making it challenging to handle market changes while keeping long-term goals in mind. Rather than reacting to short-term market swings, it is critical to develop and stick to a well-defined investing strategy.

3. Lack of Knowledge: Managing your own portfolio demands knowledge and expertise in a wide range of investing options and methods, and keeping up with market trends, financial news, and individual security performance can be tough. Continuous education and study are essential to make sound investment selections.

4. Time commitment: Managing a portfolio involves ongoing monitoring, research, and analysis, which can be time-consuming, particularly if you have a diverse range of investments. To successfully manage your portfolio, you must devote sufficient time and resources.

5. Behavioral biases can influence investment decisions; being aware of these biases and actively working to mitigate them is critical in successfully managing your portfolio.

6. Transaction costs: Transaction costs related to purchasing and selling shares, such as brokerage fees or bid-ask spreads, can accumulate and reduce your returns. When making investment decisions, it is vital to consider the influence of transaction costs.

7. Risk management is an important aspect of portfolio management. Diversification, asset allocation, and risk assessment are all critical components of effective portfolio management. Finding the right mix of risk and profit can be tricky.

Before selecting to manage your own portfolio, you must first comprehend these difficulties and assess your own abilities, time commitment, and degree of comfort. If you are feeling overwhelmed or lack the necessary experience, consider seeking professional assistance or chatting with a financial counselor.

Chapter 8

A life of gold

A prudent guide to buying your obligations

While the focus is usually on assets that generate revenue or increase in value, purchasing liabilities can also be a smart decision if done right. Here are some important factors to consider while purchasing liabilities:

1. Understand your goals and requirements for getting a liability. Are you looking for convenience, to better your lifestyle, or to use it to your advantage in the future? Clarify your goals and priorities to guide your decision-making.

2. Determine your budget and whether you can afford the liability comfortably without jeopardizing your financial stability or long-term goals, taking into account not only the initial purchase but also ongoing expenses like maintenance, insurance, and fees.

3. Gather information about the liability you are contemplating, such as the particular product or service, its quality, reputation, and potential return on investment, to make an informed selection. Look for testimonials, expert advice, and comparison studies.

4. Cost versus value: Consider the value that the liability will bring to your life or business, taking into account factors such as efficiency, quality, durability, and overall return on investment. Determine whether the advantages outweigh the costs of ownership.

5. Examine your financing options, such as loans, leases, or payment plans, and compare interest rates and terms to ensure that the financing is appropriate for your financial status and goals.

6. Consider the opportunity cost: Understand the trade-offs involved in purchasing a liability and decide whether the investment is worthwhile in the long run.

7. If you are unsure about the potential risks, returns, or repercussions of acquiring a liability, seek professional counsel.

A financial advisor or specialist in the appropriate industry can offer insights and recommend alternatives to help you make an informed decision.

Keep in mind that liabilities usually have ongoing costs and may not increase in value. Consider your financial situation, goals, and risk tolerance before making any major purchase. Due diligence and careful analysis can help guarantee that purchasing liabilities correspond with your overall financial strategy and improve your overall well-being.

Making purchases for the future

Planning for future purchases, whether for a long-awaited vacation, a new car, a home, or even minor items, is a sensible financial decision. Planning ahead of time can help you avoid impulse purchases, decrease financial stress, and make informed decisions, but it takes serious consideration and financial planning.

1. Set goals: Whether it's a new car, a dream vacation, or a down payment on a house, clearly outline your objectives to guide your planning process.

2. Investigate and estimate costs: Investigate and estimate the costs associated with your planned purchases, taking into account elements such as the purchase price, taxes, continuing maintenance or ownership fees, and any other expenditures that may be involved. Estimate how much money you will need to save to reach your objectives.

3. Create a calendar for when you want to make these purchases so you know how much time you have to save and plan accordingly.

4. Create a savings strategy: Make a plan to save money for future purchases. Determine how much you need to save each month or paycheck in order to reach your goals in the time frame you desire. Set up automatic transfers to a chosen savings account to automate these savings.

5. Examine your current budget and identify places where you might cut back on spending to free up more funds for future purchases. To expedite your savings, prioritize your expenditure and eliminate non-essential products.

6. If your desired purchase is large and you require additional funds, consider financing options such as loans or credit cards, but carefully review the conditions and interest rates to ensure they align with your financial goals.

7. Track your progress: Keep track of your savings efforts for future purchases, and evaluate your budget and savings strategy on a monthly basis to ensure you're on track and making any necessary adjustments.

8. Re-evaluate your objectives and priorities: Because life circumstances and financial goals change over time, reassess your goals and priorities on a frequent basis to ensure they still apply to your current situation, and adapt your plans as necessary.

Remember, be patient and disciplined during the planning process; saving for larger items may take time, but with consistent effort and a well-defined plan, you should be able to achieve your future purchase goals.

Conclusion.

We started with an empty lot and have since built foundations, and pillars, and even adorned the exquisite interiors of our financial home. As we stand at the crossroads of our financial journey, looking back on the path we've blazed, it's evident that building wealth is more than just amassing assets; it's an art, a dance between discipline and desire, plan and spontaneity.

Keep in mind, however, that the genuine substance of wealth can be discovered in its journey: the lessons learned, the failures conquered, and the triumphs achieved. The blueprint you now possess is more than a guide; it is a tribute to human ambition, resilience, and the age-old pursuit of riches.

As you end this book, keep in mind that wealth, in all of its forms, is a dynamic and adaptable phenomenon. Detours, new routes, and unexpected landmarks will appear on your plan; welcome them all. The actual thrill of building money is found in the twists and turns, surprises, and discoveries.

The roadmap to constructing wealth

May your journey be rich in experiences, plentiful in rewards, and, most importantly, guided by the compass of purpose and passion. Here's to not only accumulating wealth but also leaving a lasting legacy.